FRANK LLOYD WRIGHT IN ARIZONA

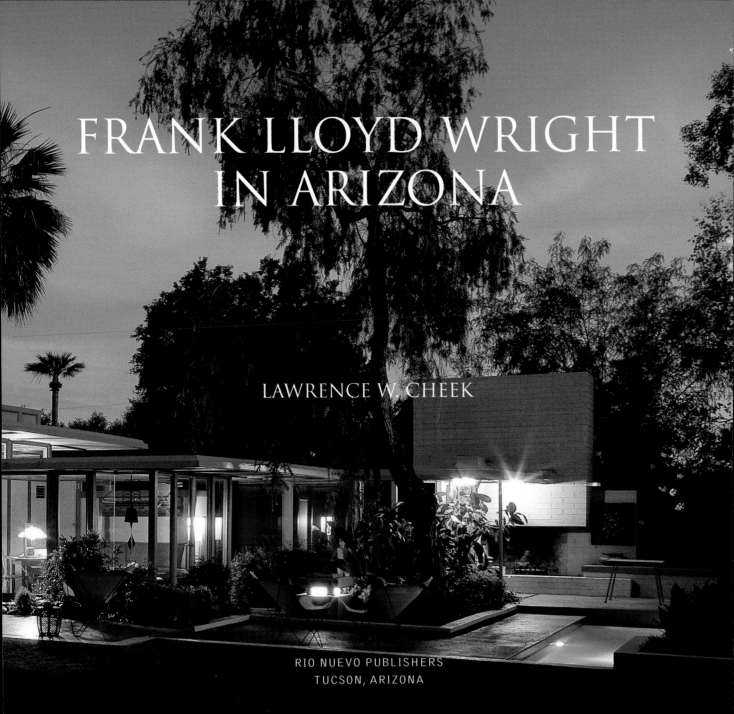

FRANK LLOYD WRIGHT
IN ARIZONA

LAWRENCE W. CHEEK

RIO NUEVO PUBLISHERS
TUCSON, ARIZONA

Rio Nuevo Publishers®
P.O. Box 5250, Tucson, Arizona 85703-0250
(520) 623-9558, www.rionuevo.com

Library of Congress Cataloging-in-Publication Data

Cheek, Larry.
Frank Lloyd Wright in Arizona / Lawrence W. Cheek.
     p. cm.
Includes bibliographical references.
ISBN-13: 978-1-887896-82-5 (hardcover)
ISBN-10: 1-887896-82-1 (hardcover)
1. Wright, Frank Lloyd, 1867-1959—Criticism and interpretation. 2. Architecture—Arizona—20th century. 3. Wright, Frank Lloyd, 1867-1959—Last years. I. Wright, Frank Lloyd, 1867-1959. II. Title.
NA737.W7C47 2006
720'.92—dc22
                                2005021037
Design: Karen Schober

Printed in Korea.
10 9 8 7 6 5 4 3

THIS BOOK IS
DEDICATED TO ELLEN PERRY
BERKELEY, WHO HAS LONG
ILLUMINATED MY WRITING ON
ARCHITECTURE. FOR THEIR
GENEROUS HELP IN RESEARCH,
THANKS TO: KAMAL AMIN,
SARA HAMMOND, BEVERLY
HART, FRANK HENRY, JOHN
MEUNIER, BRUCE BROOKS
PFEIFFER, ARNOLD ROY,
MARGO STIPE, AND
VERN SWABACK.

CONTENTS

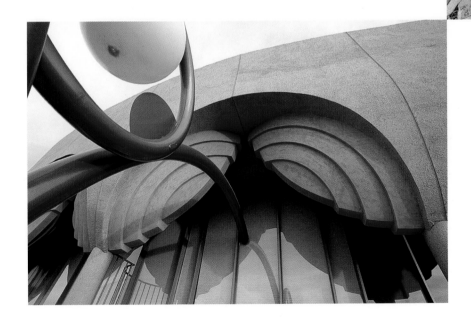

CHAPTER ONE

THE "VAST BATTLEGROUND" OF ARIZONA

AUDACIOUS, OUTRAGEOUS, FLAMBOYANT, combative, mischievous, pithy, brilliant, cockamamie, and ever eager for publicity, Frank Lloyd Wright always made good copy, which is undoubtedly why it occurred to *Phoenix Gazette* reporter Lloyd Clark to mail Wright a rendering of the proposed new Arizona state capitol, asking for comment. This was 1957, and Wright was eighty-nine years old and spending his twentieth season at his increasingly comfortable "winter camp" of Taliesin West, northeast of Phoenix. He was still prodigiously active; within the year he would design the Marin County Civic Center and fly to Baghdad to undertake a commission for a constellation of cultural monuments, and he was thoroughly enjoying his reign as America's grand old man of architecture and oracle-at-large. On the state capitol issue, though, he was unusually subdued. He replied to Clark:

Why comment? The thing is its own comment on Arizona.

—Sincerely Yours, F.LL.W.

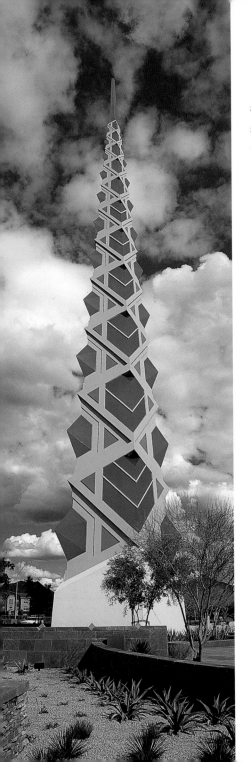

The reporter sniffed a better story, so he called Taliesin West and scored a personal appointment with Wright. As Clark later recalled it, Wright sketched an alternative capitol building on the spot, then tossed the paper into a wastebasket. Within a week or two, however, Wright decided to revisit the capitol issue in one of his traditional Sunday breakfast discussions at Taliesin West. Then-apprentice Kamal Amin, now an architect and structural engineer in Phoenix, remembers it vividly. "He had some brilliant comments with genuine, heartfelt concern about the future of our civilization if we continued to remain blind to the constant assault on the environment by expediency," Amin recalled. "Then he said, 'All right, boys, let us go to the drafting room and draw it.' We followed him into the drafting room and surrounded his desk, and in about two hours he had sketched plans and elevations for the capitol."

Warming to the prospect of actually designing the capitol for his adopted state, Wright quickly printed 20,000 promotional fliers offering his alternative "to the citizens of Arizona" with the kind of grandiose verbal flourish that had, like the luxuriant white hair and dapper suits, become his trademark.

> *Therefore no more Nineteenth Century building for Arizona to go with the mortgage already foreclosed upon her landscape by the "developer," the pole-and-wire men and political slaves-of-the-Expedient … I present a true Twentieth Century economical building of a character suited to grace Arizona landscape … that would stand in modern times for Arizona as the Alhambra once stood in Spain before our continent was discovered.*

Wright's capitol was an orgy of glittering spires and geometric filigree, spectacularly overindulging in the froufrou that sometimes burdened his final decade's work. More than thirty years later, critic Richard Nilsen of

The Arizona Republic gave it a virtuoso thrashing, calling it "one part Hollywood biblical epic, one part Alhambra and one part 1939 World's Fair … a capitol for the planet Mongo." Its 1957 reception had not been much more welcoming. Controversy bubbled for months, then Wright's scheme quietly died with the groundbreaking for a listless, low-budget expansion of the existing capitol building.

Had it been built, Wright's capitol would have soared high over budget, and even today would be nagging state bureaucrats with endless idiosyncracies and, in all probability, a leaky roof. But despite all the ego wrapped in it, Wright's design had sprung from a fierce conviction that the land and people deserved better than they were about to get, and it crackled with a quality that few public buildings in Arizona or elsewhere could claim, then or now: almighty, everlasting joy.

A MISUNDERSTANDING BROUGHT FRANK LLOYD WRIGHT to Arizona for the first time in the winter of 1928–29. Phoenix was then a city of fewer than 50,000 people, just awakening from its sleepy beginnings as a farm town majoring in citrus and cotton, and a refuge for health seekers suffering from lung diseases. Ambitious boosters were realizing the city had a prodigious future as a winter resort destination. Among them were the brothers Warren, Charles, and Albert Chase McArthur. Warren and Charles owned a Dodge dealership and were investing in hotel development schemes. Albert was an architect, and he had begun his career in 1907 as an apprentice draftsman in Wright's studio in Oak Park, Illinois.

By the end of 1927 the McArthurs had corralled enough stockholders to build a million-dollar hotel, and Albert had drawn a preliminary design borrowing the "textile block" system Wright had recently devised and used

OPPOSITE PAGE: The Arizona state capitol spire, realized in 2002 as an ornament for a Scottsdale shopping strip.

One of the Arizona Biltmore's guest cottages, almost certainly Wright-designed.

in four California houses. The patterned concrete blocks were "woven" together with hidden reinforcing rods, forming both an elegantly textured skin and a structural skeleton for the building. Albert assumed that Wright owned a patent on the system, so he offered his former employer a $10,000 fee for using it. Wright wired a quick reply, not only accepting the offer, but adding, "should come out to help you start perhaps."

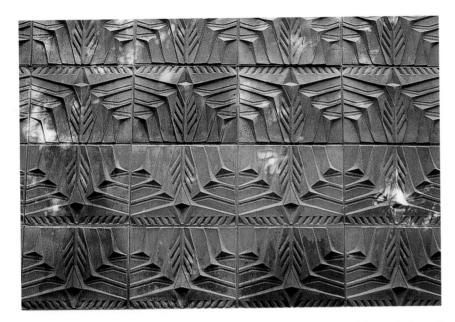

Palm fronds inspired the abstract pattern of the Arizona Biltmore's concrete blocks.

Albert had misgivings, as would anyone with firsthand knowledge of Wright's commanding ego, but he felt on balance that Wright might be helpful, so he offered a consulting salary of $1,000 a month plus the license fee for the block system. In fact, Wright had no patent and little hands-on experience with the blocks. His son Lloyd, also an architect, had supervised the California houses' construction. But Wright desperately needed the income; he had won no significant commissions since 1924.

How much Frank Lloyd Wright lies embedded in the Arizona Biltmore design has been debated for decades, but a practiced eye can make a good calculation with a visit to the hotel and a between-the-lines reading of Wright's and the McArthurs' memoirs. Throughout construction in 1928–29, rumors swirled that Wright had been the real designer, which naturally infuriated Albert McArthur—the Biltmore was arguably the most impressive building to arise in Arizona since the Spanish mission of San Xavier del Bac, completed in 1797. Albert either convinced or coerced Wright to write a public disavowal, which was published in *The*

Architectural Record. "Albert McArthur is the architect of that building," Wright wrote. "All attempts to take the credit for that performance from him are gratuitous and beside the mark."

But Wright, the sly fox, was pitching a poison dart while seeming magnanimous. In fact *he* was furious that McArthur had turned the textile block system into a mere decorative epidermis—behind the block walls a conventional steel and concrete frame held sway—and added a fourth story, which in Wright's view ruined the proportions. Wright's 1932 autobiography is plenty candid: "Having no authority myself beyond bullying Albert, making unofficial threats and suggestions behind the scenes, I was powerless to prevent this tragic waste …" Albert won only an airy dismissal: "Like rich men's sons, [he] did not much like work."

Wright probably executed a few significant pieces of the complex. The grand, two-hundred-foot-long lobby interior has a dignified but insistent visual rhythm that carries Wright's DNA, and the elegant guest cottages strewn behind the main building are built with a long one-story wing punching through a stubbier two-story block at a right angle—a Wright gesture as clear as his signature. One more broad hint: Without explicitly claiming the credit, Wright's autobiography praises the "attractive cottages" while scorning the rest of the complex.

Wright lasted just four months on the Biltmore job, but his permanent connection to Arizona locked in through an offer from an even more ambitious developer, an erstwhile veterinarian named Dr. Alexander Chandler.

While Wright was toiling semi-anonymously on the Biltmore, Chandler drove up to Phoenix from his eponymous town to meet him. The two clicked immediately; their soaring ambitions meshed perfectly. Chandler told Wright that he'd been searching ten years for an architect worthy of a spectacular foothill site he owned south of Phoenix. Wright praised Chandler as "a man of superior taste, judgment and character." When Chandler drove him out to the site, on the southern slope of what is now

OPPOSITE PAGE: Wright's sense of visual rhythm and rich textures clearly influenced the Arizona Biltmore's lobby.

Phoenix's South Mountain Park, Wright was stunned. "There could be nothing more inspiring to an architect on this earth than [this] spot of pure Arizona desert … at last here was the time, the place, and in Dr. Chandler the man." Next to Chandler's San-Marcos-in-the-Desert, the Biltmore would look like a boutique hotel.

"We had a sweeping view all around us of this vast battle-ground of titanic natural forces, called Arizona."

Arizona was intervening in Wright's life following a colossal pileup of tragedies and troubles. In 1914 a deranged servant at Taliesin, the Wright family compound at Spring Green, Wisconsin, murdered Wright's mistress Mamah Cheney, her two children, three employees, and an employee's son, and then torched the house. In 1922 Wright's long-estranged first wife, Catherine, finally agreed to a divorce; Wright promptly married the apparently psychotic Miriam Noel, who soon rendered his life a living hell. When Wright had a child with another young lover, he encountered a legal hailstorm and even spent two nights in a Minneapolis jail on charges of adultery and transporting a woman across state lines for immoral purposes. In 1926 a Wisconsin bank foreclosed on Taliesin and literally kicked the Wright clan out. The California houses were plagued with problems from leaky roofs to blow-ups with their clients. Newspapers trumpeted all these escapades to the world; the swirl of sex, violence, and financial scandal in one flamboyant celebrity package was irresistible.

Apart from the axe murders at Taliesin, many of Wright's troubles were of his own design. He was breathtakingly arrogant, financially irresponsible, and blithely deceitful whenever it served what he believed to be his higher moral calling. But he could also be dazzlingly charming, generous, and kind. Bruce Brooks Pfeiffer, the long-time Taliesin Fellowship archivist and scholar, tells a story about a twelve-year-old boy who wrote Wright in 1956 requesting a doghouse design for Eddie, his Labrador retriever. The world's most famous architect drew a floor plan and elevation on the back of the letter and returned it. Eddie soon slept in a Frank Lloyd Wright doghouse.

Wright fell in love with the desert quickly and profoundly. It was a vast, blank canvas on which he could impose his vision, unconstrained by the surroundings of a built-up city; and it was an open-air warehouse of natural forms, colors, and textures that both delighted and inspired him. Wright can be charged with many inconsistencies and hypocrisies in his life and work, but his devotion and deference to Nature—he always spelled it with a capital N—never wavered. His sermons on "organic architecture" could be a murky tumble of words, but his buildings explain the concept perfectly. They pay homage to the landscape not only in form and texture, but also in mood and spirit.

In January of 1929, Chandler invited Wright to bring his family and draftsmen back to Arizona to finish designing San-Marcos-in-the-Desert on site. The telegram arrived at Taliesin during a howling blizzard, the temperature twenty-two below zero, and Wright's response was understandably enthusiastic. A party of fifteen bundled up and hastily fled Wisconsin in a car caravan. On arrival in Phoenix, Wright considered the expense of housing his troupe in apartments for the winter and abruptly decided to build a camp instead. Chandler offered some of his land, and Wright was so enraptured with it that he and his "boys," as he invariably called his apprentices, began building the next morning. Wright christened the camp "Ocatillo," misspelling the name of the spidery, spring-flowering shrub that flourished on the site.

Wright devoted several pages of his autobiography to this transient collection of shelters, which is a clue to its pivotal significance in his life and work. The site, now smudged over by suburban development near Interstate 10 and Chandler Boulevard, inspired him to poetic eloquence: "We had a sweeping view all around us of this vast battleground of titanic natural forces, called Arizona." He quickly absorbed its implications for architecture: "obvious symmetry" was wrong, as were flat, sun-splashed wall surfaces. In fact, just about everything that had been built in Arizona was unsuited for it:

To see unspoiled native character insulted like this! Arizona character seems to cry out for a space-loving architecture of its own. The straight line and flat plane, sun-lit, must come here—of all places—but they should become the dotted line, the broad, low, extended plane textured because in all this astounding desert there is not one hard undotted line to be seen.

And although he designed Ocatillo's temporary cabins in a day, he considered it an important design exercise for himself and a lesson for anyone who followed:

I believe we pay too slight attention to making slight buildings beautiful or beautiful buildings slight. Lightness and strength may now become synonymous terms.

Even though it was just a temporary camp, photos of Ocatillo were published in architectural magazines worldwide.

Lloyd Wright, Frank's oldest son, plays the piano at Ocatillo.

"Ocatillo"!—little desert camp—you are "ephemera." Nevertheless you shall drop a seed or two yourself in course of time—on ground now needlessly barren.

Ocatillo consisted of fifteen wood cabins with asymmetrical white canvas roofs and scarlet canvas flaps in lieu of windows. Wright claimed to love the "agreeable diffusion of light" that the translucent canvas afforded, but it was also economic necessity—without a Chandler check yet in hand, the Wright clan was broke. Still, the cabins accomplished something that no Anglo-American architecture in the Southwest had done up to this time: they harmonized with the land by abstracting nature's own forms, in this case the pointy mountain ridgelines and triangular cross-sections of the slopes. The triangular flaps also echoed the flamelike spring flowers of the ocotillo.

San-Marcos-in-the-Desert erupted from Wright's pencils as nothing less than an entire visual vocabulary and ethic for building in the desert. An immense and majestic building, it seemed to slip into its site with as little

Textured and creased wall surfaces of San-Marcos-in-the-Desert were intended to scatter and diffuse the harsh sunlight.

disturbance as a hawk alighting in a tree. The three-story guest wings stairstepped back, breaking up the apparent mass of the façade into human-scaled heights and providing each room with its own south-facing sun terrace on the roof of the room below. The vertical ribbing of the concrete blocks recalled the fluted torsos of saguaro cacti, and the ornamental triangles in the tower saluted South Mountain in the background. "The entire building is in pattern an abstraction of this mountain region itself," Wright wrote, then added, a little too magnificently, "a human habitation to live in as long maybe as the mountain behind it lasts."

Nature may have perked up her ears at this pinprick of hubris. A few months later the stock market crashed and Chandler's fortune collapsed.

AN MARCOS IN THE DESERT   FOR   ALEXANDER CHANDLER · FRANK LL

The hotel never got built, Chandler was able to pay Wright only $2,500 of the promised $40,000 fee, and as if to add inhospitality to injury, local Indians—Wright assumed this, at least—carted off Ocatillo's remnants for shelter or firewood the following winter.

Wright seemed to accept the turns of misfortune with surprising grace; one senses that the two seasons in the desert had kindled some fresh optimism in him. "Never mind," he wrote. "Something had started that was not stopping thus. Later you will see consequences as this record proceeds." He bought a used Packard sport phaeton "wide open to the sky" and led his caravan back to Wisconsin.

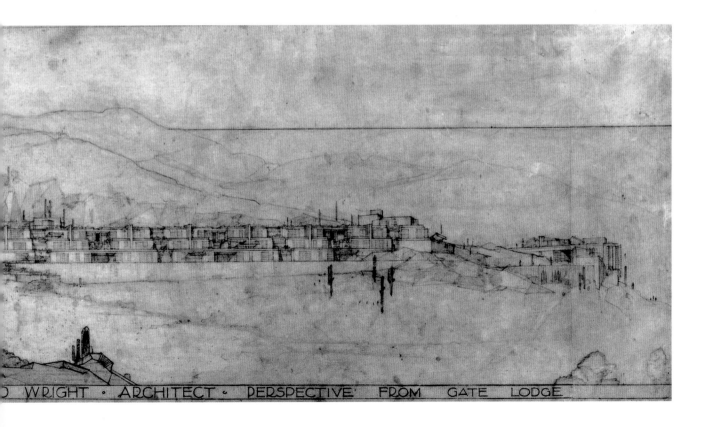

WRIGHT · ARCHITECT · PERSPECTIVE · FROM GATE LODGE

CHAPTER TWO

THE "SPIRITUAL CATHARTIC"

THE GREAT DEPRESSION SHRIVELED WRIGHT'S PRACTICE, as it did nearly every American architect's. But Wright's third marriage (to Olga Ivanovna Milanov, who he always called "Olgivanna") was, at last, a supportive and fulfilling partnership; he had the Taliesin Fellowship, the circle of idealistic young apprentices that he and Olgivanna founded in 1932; and as always, his mind churned with a relentless traffic of ideas to loose upon the world. The most ambitious of these was Broadacre City, an anti-urban utopia that called for redesign of the entire concept of American cities.

In the winter of 1934–35, Chandler, still enchanted with Wright, offered the fellowship a converted polo stable for winter living quarters where they could refine the Broadacre City concept. The entourage loaded a tottering truck with Depression-era provisions—home-canned vegetables and barrels of sauerkraut—and trundled back to Arizona, where they built a twelve-by-twelve-foot model of Broadacre City that would later go on exhibition at Rockefeller Center. Apprentice Eugene Masselink spoke

of the group's gratitude for the reprieve from Wisconsin's winter: "There is quiet repose about the atmosphere and a freshness in the air. Never have I breathed or lived such boundless purity of space." Not that it was the perfect idyll. "Toward the end of our stay our supplies ran out," recalled fellow Cornelia Brierly, "and we subsisted mostly on sauerkraut, salt pork, and peanut butter."

Back in frigid Wisconsin the next winter, Wright contracted pneumonia. A physician told Olgivanna that if Wright would spend every winter in Arizona, it would prolong his life by twenty years. Since Wright was already sixty-eight this was either kindly optimism or eerie prescience. They took the advice; Wright lived another twenty-three years, and they turned out to be the most astoundingly productive of his life.

The Wrights left Taliesin on Christmas Eve of 1937 to prospect for raw land in the Phoenix area. In early January they visited a site at the foot of the McDowell Mountains ten miles north of Scottsdale. It bristled with prickly but remarkably lush vegetation—barrel and saguaro cacti, staghorn and jumping cholla, bursage, mesquite, palo verde, and ironwood. Quartzite boulders littered the site in a geological rainbow of colors— violet, russet, gray, and charcoal. The prehistoric Hohokam had lived here; there were enigmatic petroglyphs and grinding stones for corn. Wright grasped the site's possibilities instantly and instinctively. Olgivanna described the moment:

OVERLEAF: Cholla cacti punctuate the landscape surrounding Taliesin West.
RIGHT: "The boys" renovate the roof at Taliesin West, 1947.

We had to stop the car and go on by foot. It was very wild, there were no trails, our feet full of cactus, and we were always stopping every few minutes. The desert at first appeared to me too bare, too abstract, after coming from Wisconsin. But then it had a magnetic power ... that overcomes you, and it overcame Frank. "Oh," he said, "we have got to build here, this is pure abstraction wherever you look."

Wright wasted no time. He bought the first parcel of what eventually would total nearly six hundred acres, and wired the fellowship in Wisconsin:

Wright found prehistoric Hohokam petroglyphs on the Taliesin West property and integrated them into the compound.

...BRING SHOVELS, RAKES, HOES, AND ALSO HOSE. EIGHT-
EEN DRAFTING BOARDS AND TOOLS. WHEELBARROW, CON-
CRETE MIXER, SMALL HOHLER (ELECTRICAL PLANT) AND
WIRE, MELODEON, OIL STOVES FOR COOKING AND HEAT-
ING, WATER HEATER, VIOLA, CELLO, RUGS NOT IN USE AND
WHATEVER ELSE WE NEED.

The shovel- and cello-wielding fellowship would need water, of course,
and the site was miles from the nearest tentacles of civilization. This
was blessed isolation for Wright, who reviled cities as "vampires,"
"tumors," and "monster leviathans." But he had gambled precipitously
on finding groundwater under his desert. A driller was hired to sink a
well, and after some anxious days, it produced—at the frightening
depth of 486 feet! According to a story that still circulates around Taliesin West—and it might be cautioned here that some Wright stories
exude the blended aromas of fact and legend—a professional dowser
later checked out the well and proclaimed that Wright "must have been
a mystic, because he chose the single best place in the McDowell Mountains to drill a well."

Wright actually set up drafting tables on the site, designing on
brown butcher paper to reduce the glare from the brilliant winter sun.
Rattlesnakes slithered about and flash floods tumbled off the mountain,
but Wright took it all in stride—these hazards all had their rightful
place in Nature, and were to be respected and learned from. When com-
plaints arose, Wright would tut-tut: "We must strengthen the spiritual
muscle." More than ever, he was assuming the mantle of spiritual leader,
one who inspired a quasi-religious devotion within the circle. In a
remarkably revealing passage from her unpublished autobiography,
Olgivanna recalled an overnight camping trip to the nearby Superstition
Mountains:

When night came, Frank found a smooth place for me beside a huge flat rock on which he spread his sleeping bag. He was soon asleep while I was adjusting to the atmosphere of the mountain. The moonlight was so brilliant and the thrill of the mysterious mountain so overpowering that I did not fall asleep for a long time. When I looked at Frank, he was stretched out full length on his back, his noble profile appeared carved out of the rock, as an image of some god that men of ancient times worshipped.

For the apprentices, life at Taliesin West-in-the-making strengthened more than their spiritual muscles. The hardest work, one apprentice recalled, was convincing the site to host a building. Just below the sandy surface soil was a layer of caliche, hard as cement (a natural deposit of calcium carbonate common in arid land, caliche essentially *is* cement), and the apprentices had nothing but picks and shovels for the attack. The fellowship's lone machine was a concrete mixer. But the caliche proved so hard that Wright figured the buildings could manage without foundations, to save money. The entire compound, now more than sixty years old, simply rests on bare ground.

For wall material, Wright had his "boys" raid the site for those colorful quartzite boulders and mine the arroyos for sand. These became what Wright called "desert rubble stone," which not only cost nothing, but also harmonized in color and texture with the surrounding landscape. It *was* the surrounding landscape, rearranged and propped up to make shelter. Wright, the construction superintendent as well as the architect, was exacting. The boulders weren't just heaved into the forms; Wright directed their placement, stone by stone, then had the apprentices wire them in place, tilt the forms upright, and pour the cement around them. Frugality was ever the watchword. Once a wall was in place, the plywood forms would be broken down and re-used for another form. "When the pieces finally got too small, we'd burn them in a fifty-five-gallon drum to keep

OPPOSITE PAGE: The family living room at Taliesin West offers luxurious daylight and views, but less-than-luxurious Wright-designed seating.

warm," recalled former apprentice Arnold Roy. The apprentices' memoirs never mention it, but the penny-pinching surely struck them as ironic, because Wright was a legendary profligate with his clients' money. (The 1939 Johnson Wax complex in Racine, Wisconsin, ended up costing *several times* the original estimate.)

But Wright did not conceive of Taliesin West as a palace. It was a winter camp—like Ocatillo, it originally had white canvas roofs and canvas flaps instead of glass windows—and his architectural laboratory. Every winter, he would direct the "boys" in a blizzard of modifications and additions. (Glass arrived in 1945, after years of Olgivanna's pleading.) But never did it seem to sprawl, overwhelm its site, or violate its fundamental premise of a building in perfect tune with the spirit and form of the land around it. And it was that great rarity in architecture, a creation that owed no debt to any building ever made before, not even in the architect's own *oeuvre*. Wright's words ring absolutely true: "The design sprang out of itself, with no precedent and nothing following it."

Likewise, there was no precedent for the form of architectural education that occurred at Taliesin West (and at the original Taliesin in Wisconsin). It was both more and less than a classic apprenticeship: *more* in that the "boys" furnished the labor for every aspect of living at the summer and winter Taliesins, from gardening to cooking to patching chronically leaky roofs, and were expected to attend a remarkable spectrum of lectures, films, and concerts. Black ties were mandatory on Sunday evenings; the running joke was that you needed to bring just four things to Taliesin West: a sleeping bag, a flashlight, a hammer, and a tuxedo. Many of the fellows played instruments themselves; Wright cherished music and always managed to have a grand piano at his disposal wherever he alighted, even in his rustic wedge at Ocatillo.

And *less*: Wright offered no formal teaching program. The students were expected to learn by watching, absorbing, and transmuting his

"The spiritual cathartic that was the desert worked—swept the spirit clean of stagnant ways and habitual forms ready for fresh adventure."

sketches into working drawings. Wright's preeminent biographer, Brendan Gill, has pointed out that this form of education had one fundamental defect: Wright was a genius, and geniuses are by definition inimitable. His redeeming quality was his willingness to pass on whatever he knew, which seemed boundless. He once spotted Arnold Roy splattering himself while painting a ceiling at Taliesin in Wisconsin. "Young, man, *this* is the way you paint!" Wright said, taking the brush and demonstrating. Dressed immaculately, as usual, Wright got no paint on himself. "From that day on, I learned to be a very clean painter," Roy said. "It was an incredible knowledge the man had of every kind of endeavor and it wasn't a superficial knowledge. He really knew every craft that was involved in the art of architecture."

Depression-era apprentices paid an annual tuition of $1,100 and furnished the Wrights with several times that value in labor. Their attraction (and devotion) to the master grew from their feverish conviction that Wright's ideas pointed the only way for a modern architecture to emerge from flowery nineteenth-century historicism. The severe, machinelike, anti-humanistic ethic of Bauhaus design then emanating from Europe appalled them, as it did Wright. They also tended to be intrepid souls, and the adventure of an apprenticeship with Frank Lloyd Wright ratcheted even higher with the birth of Taliesin West.

Each November the Wrights and their "boys" would flee Wisconsin in a motley caravan, Wright's luxury car (one of his many insatiable indulgences) leaving the others behind in a hobbling parade of clattering rods, dead batteries, and flat tires. Cherokee red was Wright's favorite color, and it reveals something about the nature of the fellowship that nearly all the fellows painted their jalopies red, too. To save money along the way, the fellows would camp out, or one would rent a tourist court cabin and sneak the others inside to bathe and sleep. Few of them had ever imagined living in such an exotic environment as Arizona offered, especially with the intimacy that the "winter camp" provided. Cornelia Brierly:

Living in tents kept us close to desert life. At night we checked our tents for rattlesnakes and our sleeping bags for scorpions, kissing bugs, or black widow spiders. Often we encountered packrats, skinks, ring-tailed cats, rock squirrels, and deer. Sometimes in the dark we would bump into a wild burro. After a rain we enjoyed the fresh smell of creosote bush as we explored local canyons and mountains …

Every synapse in Wright's creative imagination was tingling at the acquaintance of this new environment, and it must have been valuable for the apprentices, too. Wright gave frequent credit to the desert as inspiration and teacher:

The Arizona desert is no place for the hard box-walls of the houses of the Middle West and East. Here all is sculptured by wind and water, patterned in color and texture. Rocks and reptiles no less so than the cacti. A desert building should be nobly simple in outline as the region itself is sculptured: should have learned from the cactus many secrets of straight-line-patterns for its forms, playing with the light and softening the building into its proper place among the organic desert creations— the man-made building heightening the beauty of the desert and the desert more beautiful because of the building.

And Wright's architecture became—if not necessarily more beautiful— more daring, more exuberant than ever. In a 1949 essay published in *Arizona Highways* Wright revealed:

The spiritual cathartic that was the desert worked—swept the spirit clean of stagnant ways and habitual forms ready for fresh adventure.

OPPOSITE PAGE: The pond and arch at Taliesin West echo the "stark geometry" Wright admired in the surrounding desert landscape.

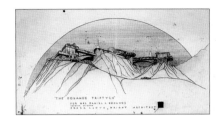

LEFT: The Pauson residence in Phoenix contrasted strong horizontal and vertical forms, a Wright trademark. Fire destroyed it in 1941. RIGHT: The unbuilt Donahoe Triptych recapped a graded mountain peak with a main residence, with bridges extending to two guest houses.

CHAPTER THREE

AN ARCHITECTURE FOR ARIZONA

FRANK LLOYD WRIGHT'S CONTRIBUTION TO ARCHITECTURE is too broad, too deep, and too omnifarious to be easily explained, and yet anyone who has a passing familiarity with it can instantly recognize his work. More than a style, it is a suite of principles—peppered, for good measure, by uniquely Wrightian idiosyncracies.

He broke the box, casting off the concept of architecture as container, instead shaping buildings to express the spaces inside them, and later creating forms that approached the expressiveness of pure sculpture. He manipulated interior space to create mood and drama. He put geometry to dazzling work, taking a basic theme of a building—wedge, triangle, circle—and spinning out its ornamentation as variations on that theme. He grasped the liberating possibilities of the twentieth century's new structural materials, steel and concrete, more thoroughly than his more formally educated contemporaries. He believed that materials should express themselves boldly and honestly.

Most importantly of all, he envisioned buildings as creations that should embrace—and be embraced by—the landscape, not foreign objects to be imposed on their sites. The color, texture, and topography of the land, and the orientation and quality of the sunlight, should deeply inform every building's design. This he considered a matter of morality rather than mere aesthetic philosophy, and he endlessly proselytized it—he was the son and grandson of preachers, after all—to a world that saw him variously as inspiring, brilliant, exasperating, and out of touch with reality.

In the end, though, there are the buildings—amazing creations to be savored and learned from.

I have experienced a handful of magical moments in architecture, when a man-made environment gave me an unforgettable emotional shiver, and one of them occurred while visiting the drafting studio at Taliesin West more than twenty years ago. The original canvas roof had long since been replaced with translucent acrylic for better durability and insulation, but the effect of the diffused natural light was still just as Wright intended. A fluffy cloud drifted across the sun, and the mood of the room suddenly darkened, like one of those unexpected and ominous major-to-minor key changes in a Schubert piano sonata. My mood shifted too, suddenly introspective. Why, I wondered for some time afterward, would one want a quality of light that changed with the weather, the time of day and even the season, in a work room? Well, maybe because work *should* be affected by emotion and a connection to the cadences of nature. We are not machines.

More than any of the mid-twentieth century's other pathbreaking architects—Mies van der Rohe, Le Corbusier, Louis Kahn, Alvar Aalto, Eero Saarinen—Wright's work was user-friendly and approachable, designed as much for the ordinary person as the connoisseur. For all their wizardry, his buildings never seem intimidating—you walk in and immediately feel welcome. You sense the humanity of the architecture, rather than the presence of an aloof and unapproachable genius.

Not counting his input on the Biltmore, Wright designed twelve buildings or complexes that arose in Arizona during his lifetime or after. One
more house, the Lykes residence in Phoenix, existed only in rough sketch
form by Wright—he was starting on it the day he died. Taliesin Fellowship
architect John Rattenbury completed it, and the result is so Wrightian that

*The circle-and-arc motif of the Lykes
residence includes kitchen cabinets and
built-in seating that curve with the walls.*

it deserves honorary addition to the list. Two of the completed works, Ocatillo and the Pauson House, were demolished, and another, the Pieper house, has been altered so much that it hardly counts as Wright's work today. The Arizona State Capitol spire has appeared, spectacularly but incongruously, beside a Scottsdale restaurant. Another twenty-five Arizona projects were not built, either because their clients ran into financial difficulties or didn't like what Wright offered them.

The Pieper residence, built in 1952, has since been substantially remodeled.

That leaves eleven buildings—Taliesin West, an auditorium, a church, the spire, and seven houses (or eight, if you include one that was completed after Wright's death)—standing today, and the most astounding thing is how different from each other they all are, and yet how clearly they are the creations of the same man.

———

A TOUR OF WRIGHT'S ARIZONA WORK rightly begins at the fountainhead, **Taliesin West.** One of Scottsdale's most celebrated tourist attractions, it welcomes 125,000 visitors a year for a varied menu of guided tours and occasional symposiums. The compound has been changed substantially though respectfully since Wright's death—new materials, interior rearrangements, and several posthumous structures on the grounds—but since Wright was constantly improving it himself, there never was a "completed" version for a historic preservation reference.

The compound provokes powerful and varied reactions. "Taliesin West is strange and enigmatic," wrote Neil Levine in one of the most probing studies of Wright's architecture. Architect Pietro Belluschi said that Taliesin West, more than any of Wright's other works, "shows how to grasp the mood of the land and transform it into a place of harmony and beauty." Elizabeth Gordon, who edited *House Beautiful* and was a friend of the Wrights, sensed "a feeling of something almost prehistoric" when she visited. Wright was certainly conscious of reaching back into time when he conceived it. He had boulders with Hohokam petroglyphs installed at strategic intersections in the compound, and he wrote in his autobiography that the camp "belonged to the Arizona desert as though it had stood there during creation."

Taliesin West's buildings insinuate themselves into the land in several ways. Most obvious is the texture and slope of the stone walls, an abstraction of the mountainous horizons of Arizona. The triangular terrace

OVERLEAF: The slopes of the stone walls and rooflines soften Taliesin West's visual impact on its site. BELOW: The wedge forms the geometric motif of First Christian Church's sanctuary.

on the south is an echo of the McDowell Mountains, flattened to the ground. The strange, fin-like trusses elbowed over the drafting studio give the entire compound a defensive posture, like the body armor of a horned lizard, and yet on a winter evening when pink streaks rake the sky overhead, the armor melts into the heavens. Moving through the compound is like exploring a slot canyon on the Colorado Plateau; the walls close into

claustrophobic crannies, then unexpectedly burst into large, light-filled rooms. Theatrical, yes, but one never feels manipulated by cheap architectural tricks: Taliesin West is as honest as the landscape itself.

And just as quirky. The dozen ceramic Chinese theater tableaus installed in the walls are there for no good reason except that Wright liked them. There are many places to bash one's head. The rain gutters in the Wrights' living room run *inside*, under the ceiling. And the chairs and couches, all designed by Wright, range from barely tolerable to nearly unbearable.

First Christian Church is a spiritual cousin of Taliesin West, although its site, a luxurious sea of grass in a north Phoenix neighborhood of long, low ranch houses, is very different in character. Wright originally designed the church in 1949 as part of a seventy-three-acre desert campus outside Phoenix for Southwest Christian Seminary, which was nothing more than a gleam in an evangelist's eye. This minister, Peyton Canary, flattered and cajoled Wright into preparing presentation drawings on contingency for a fund-raising campaign. "I should like this project to be the Arizona monument to your genius, the masterpiece of your whole career," Canary told Wright. These were the perfect words to lubricate the architect's ambition. "Oh, Canary," Wright assured him, "you will get the money all right!"

The church isn't quite a great building—the desert rubble stone and triangle-and-wedge geometric theme have no mountain backdrop to second them, as Taliesin West does, and the lid-like roof at the north end rises like a rhetorical question with no forthcoming answer. But the sanctuary is a gloriously theatrical space. One approaches through a sphinctered, cavern-like passage, then the worship space suddenly explodes in light, color, and dazzling geometry—the trademark Wright technique called "compression-release." Delicious details abound. The abstract tree-form concrete columns on the sanctuary perimeter, piercing the floor-to-ceiling windows and supporting the massive roof, accomplish the nearly impossible: they're both structure and grace note. The bell tower is a virtuoso concerto of

First Christian's spire and bell tower pierce the sky.

geometric whiz-bang, a four-sided pyramid of stacked and canted trapezoids topped by a cross with little Martian baubles at the tips. It's over the top, but as a whole, the ensemble of church and tower somehow exudes serenity at the same time that it's boiling over with ideas.

LEFT: Grady Gammage Memorial Auditorium's grand tier seats 606 and spans 145 feet without support columns or contact with the back wall. The balcony above seats 682. RIGHT: Concrete scallops nestled under Gammage's arches may suggest stage curtains, but Wright intended an abstraction of palm tree trunks and fronds.

Grady Gammage Memorial Auditorium is another transplanted design, and from a rather more remote desert site: it started out as an opera house for Baghdad.

In 1957 Wright flew to Baghdad for an audience with the king of Iraq, who promptly commissioned an astonishing complex of civic buildings including an opera house, auditorium, planetarium, two art museums, several university buildings, and a colossal monument to Haroun al-Rashid, the eighth-century caliph of Baghdad immortalized in *One Thousand and One Nights*. Nowhere in recorded history had a ninety-year-old architect been handed such an ambitious project, but Wright seized it as handily as he would have forty years earlier—he was never troubled by self-doubt or any shortage of energy. The king was assassinated the next year, which conveniently dovetailed with a forthcoming commission from Arizona State University for a big auditorium. Wright adapted the Baghdad opera house, fortunately clipping off its bizarre tarantula-like spire, to the local job.

The buildings of Wright's final decade are the most controversial of his career, and Gammage (named for the university's then-president, Grady Gammage) illustrates why. The auditorium is self-consciously romantic to the point of bombast. It resembles an immense pink wedding cake festooned with sugary flourishes. Its ornaments—particularly the coppery rails and globes bounding alongside the upswept pedestrian ramps— would be at home in a sci-fi cartoon illustration from the fifties. While Taliesin West is one of Wright's most timeless designs, Gammage is anchored in its age of flamboyance and giddy excess as surely as a '59 Cadillac.

Yet, Wright at his worst is never an uninteresting or uninspired Wright, and there is much to admire in Gammage. The ornamentation is organic in that it all bubbles from the geometric theme: circles. Inside the auditorium, the circle appears in the form of sixteen frosted light globes planted in round, turquoise-colored surrounds on the side walls, where the theme becomes elegant rather than cartoonish. The seating is surprisingly intimate for a very big (3,023 seats) auditorium, and the "grand tier" balcony sweeps across the entire 145-foot-wide span of the hall without column support or contact with the back wall. Seated on this level, you can't see any of the 1,700 people seated below, and you have the sensation of sharing, say, the Philadelphia Orchestra (which inaugurated the hall in 1964) with a chamber music-sized audience. The acoustics are equally intimate. When Vladimir Horowitz played here in 1980, listeners at the back could feel the *pianissimo* notes of his Chopin like feathers brushing against the ears.

Gammage's staff say it works "extremely well" as a contemporary concert hall with one exception: as thoroughly as Wright understood the desert environment, the ground-level lobby and third-level promenade both face west, simulating solar ovens on summer evenings. Simple changes such as a shift in the orientation, or an indented lobby wall, would have made the building more welcoming.

FEW ARCHITECTS WHO ACHIEVE ANYTHING CLOSE to Wright's stature bother with designing private residences. The commissions are small, the aggravations loom large. But Wright retained a fierce and idealistic interest in the American house throughout his life, designing more than three hundred private residences. He believed fervently in the single-family home as the ultimate expression of individual liberty and insisted that people of modest

Small and simple, the Adelman residence
still exhibits fine architectural detailing.

means still had the right to expect quality. "The house of moderate cost is not only America's major architectural problem but the problem most difficult [to solve]," he wrote. The "expedient houses built by the millions" are "stupid makeshifts, putting on some style or other, really having none—no integrity."

Wright designed twenty-three houses for Arizona, most for the Phoenix area. Nine were built; seven are still in use as private residences. The Pauson Residence burned down in 1941, although its stone chimney was transplanted to serve as a symbolic gate to Alta Vista Estates, a remarkable Phoenix subdivision of houses by notable architects. The Price Residence, which was the largest of Wright's completed Arizona houses, is still privately owned (by the U-Haul International founding family) but not lived in; the company rents it out for civic, charitable, and corporate events.

Two of the most interesting houses, the **Adelman Residence** of 1951 and the **Boomer Residence** of 1953, are next-door neighbors in Alta Vista, but they are no more stylistic relatives than a Jeep and a Jaguar. Adelman is one of Wright's several dozen Usonian houses, his solution to the problem of moderate-cost housing. The Usonian houses were low, single-story houses with two intersecting wings, a carport (Wright's invention), a generous living room, and pipsqueak bedrooms. For the Adelman family, Wright devised the "Usonian Automatic" system of construction—concrete blocks that could easily be assembled, theoretically by unskilled labor, like children's Lego blocks. A succession of owners have added to the house and unfortunately encrusted the blocks with spray-on stucco.

Boomer was originally designed as a California beach house. When the client's plans fell through, Wright dusted off the design, made a few modifications, and voila!—a desert cottage of stone masonry and exposed timber beams, bristling with obtuse and acute angles that respond to the mountains on Phoenix's horizons. The stairway to the second floor is so tight that even an average-sized person has to stoop and slink, but at the top, the master bedroom appears in a dramatic eruption of space and light,

with a floor-to-ceiling prow window on the northern sky. It's a lot of drama for a cottage-sized house of 1,400 square feet, but Wright never felt that small commissions were undeserving of big ideas.

At 5,300 square feet, the **Price Residence** in Paradise Valley falls at the opposite end of the residential scale—it was a very large house in 1953, especially considering that it was intended only as a winter retreat. But the client, Harold C. Price, already knew that when you contracted with Wright, you were likely to get far more (and pay far more) than you bargained for. A few years before, Price, an Oklahoma businessman, had vis-

ited Wright at Taliesin in Wisconsin, mistakenly thinking he needed a modest three-story office building in his hometown of Bartlesville. Wright bewitched him into sponsoring an exquisite nineteen-story tower, a "needle on the prairie," which actually was a recycled scheme for an unbuilt Manhattan apartment building.

At first introduction, the Price home appears unusually formal and showy for a Wright residence. One of the ingratiating qualities of most Wright houses is that despite their fame and staggering value, an ordinary family and its clutter could move right in and feel welcomed. Here, the strict rhythm of the vaguely Egyptian concrete-block columns and the very long (170 feet!) overhanging roof maintain a rather pompous and ceremonial air. Inside, though, are some wonderfully inviting spaces. The atrium merges indoor and outdoor space, creating a thousand-square-foot room with an oculus open to the sky. In the living room, observant visitors will notice how even the natural light is, with no hot spots, no glare, and no fill-in lamps needed. This was the product of Wright's attention to detail: the eaves are wider on the south side than on the north, to balance the winter light.

The **Raymond Carlson Residence** was designed for the legendary *Arizona Highways* editor, who had become a friend of Wright's. Since the Carlsons were far from wealthy, Wright kept the construction and geometry simple and the dimensions modest—only 1,100 square feet. Redwood four-by-fours became a frame, with modular panels of gray Transite (an asbestos-cement mixture) forming the walls between. The Carlsons pitched in with their own sweat equity, prompting an astonishing gesture from Wright. "It is so finely built," he wrote, "I am giving half my fee to the builder as a reward of merit; the rest of the fee goes to Raymond himself to help furnish his aristocratic little gem of a house."

Wright designed the **David Wright Residence** for his own son, using concrete block—David had adopted the material as his business—but

OPPOSITE PAGE: The indoor-outdoor atrium of the Price residence extended living space through the Phoenix winter.

The Carlson residence demonstrated Wright's remarkable ability to innovate for clients with modest budgets.

torturing it into the form of a coil, as if to demonstrate the possibilities of the medium. The **Lykes Residence**, which existed only in sketches at Wright's death, is the most organic of all the Arizona houses for its uncanny dialogue with its site. A swarm of colliding circles launches itself from the lip of a forty-five-degree slope, balancing the gruff angularity of the hill with a sweet, flowing grace—a ballet in a boiler room. Wright could complement a landscape with either harmony or contrast. The **Jester/Pfeiffer Residence**, another study in cylinders, was commissioned by a Hollywood set designer in 1938; Taliesin scholar Bruce Brooks Pfeiffer built it in 1971 as his own residence on the Taliesin West property.

———

ONE OF WRIGHT'S UNBUILT ARIZONA HOUSES, the **Donahoe Triptych**, deserves special mention for its sheer virtuosic chutzpah. In 1959, a client named Helen Donahoe contacted Wright about a hilltop site she had bought. A previous owner had already bulldozed the top of the peak, unforgivable vandalism in Wright's world. Of all his pronouncements, the most famous, and the one to which he most religiously adhered, was that "No house should ever be *on* any hill … It should be *of* the hill, belonging to it, so hill and house could live together each the happier for the other."

As Helen Donahoe's son Michael later recalled, Wright showed up one day, sketches in hand, and announced, "I've come to put the top back on the mountain." Indeed, the main house of the Donahoe Triptych literally crowned the decapitated hill, even providing a domed "sky parlor" on the top level with 360-degree views of the valley below. Bridges then slashed through space to link the residence with two guesthouses on adjacent hills. The 17,000-square-foot project was Wright's last completed design, which he might have considered a fitting crown for his life: Frank Lloyd Wright, architect, restorer of mountains.

Another unbuilt design, the **Daylight Bank** for Tucson, illustrates how he could braid utter impracticality and amazing insight. The 1947 Valley National Bank branch was to be roofed with an enormous translucent jewel to flood the interior with diffused daylight. The infant technology of air conditioning would have been hopelessly outmatched by the summer sun. But the sweat lodge/bank included another innovation: six drive-in windows for

OVERLEAF: The low ribbon of windows in the circular Jester/Pfeiffer residence offer a landscape panorama when viewers sit down.

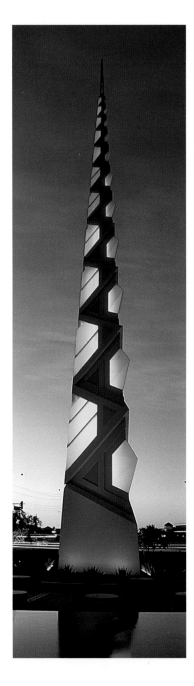

bank patrons to transact their business from their cars. According to a cherished story around the Taliesin Fellowship, the bank board scoffed at the drive-in feature, telling Wright that "no one would ever want to do that."

In 2002, the **Arizona State Capitol spire** arose in a north Scottsdale shopping strip, minus the rest of the building to which Wright would have had it attached. At night, fluorescent lights inside the 125-foot spindle emanate a soft, sapphire-blue glow through translucent acrylic panels. A private developer commissioned it as a landmark, and if financing materializes, the Daylight Bank eventually will appear beside it as a private community center, leasing space to not-for-profit organizations.

The spire is intriguing by day and even lovely at night, but it poses questions as it serves as an exclamation mark for a commercial development. Can a work of architecture, detached from its original site, function, and meaning, have any value beyond novelty? Does it contribute to the architect's reputation or our understanding of him? In the spire's case, the answers are all no. Visually, the lonely needle has to compete with the commotion of twelve lanes of traffic at its foot, and with a sprawling Scottsdale more than twenty times the size of the village Wright knew. For the spire to have the kind of landmark impact today that Wright intended, it needs to be two or three times this size, and planted in a commanding location.

Returning to Taliesin West, a Wright enthusiast has to confront another thorny question: What are the disciples doing with his legacy?

Never in history had there been an architectural career like Wright's, so it isn't surprising that the continuing enterprises following his death in 1959 were, and are, likewise unique. The Taliesin Fellowship sailed on much as it had during his life, with the seasonal shuttles between Wisconsin and Arizona, and black-tie concerts every Sunday evening. Olgivanna served as the spiritual and managerial leader until her own death in 1985. The Frank Lloyd Wright School of Architecture also continued, with the student apprentices farming, cooking, drawing, and building, almost exactly as they had under Wright. The architecture firm incorporated as Taliesin Architects persevered until 2003, bringing into being fifteen unbuilt Wright projects and doing a substantial amount of original design work, from private residences to community master plans.

Like the turmoil laced through Wright's life, not one of these activities has escaped controversy. Behind the scenes, the two Taliesins have had the air of monasteries devoted to the veneration of a saint, who is always referred to as "Mr. Wright." Many critics have dismissed Taliesin Architects' work as derivative—pale or overly mannered imitations of the master. The architects are acutely aware of the criticism, and they have struggled to break free while remaining in the service of an ideal that they have literally devoted their lives to.

"We have the problem—or perhaps the inspiration—of living in the path of a man who created almost every possible architectural form," John Rattenbury, perhaps the most gifted architect who remained with the fellowship, once admitted to me in a candid conversation. "It's easy to be bizarre; not at all easy to come up with a house on a hill that grows naturally out of that hill, and do it in a form that Mr. Wright didn't already think of. Every one of us here would give our eyeteeth to be able to design a building, then have the others come up and say, 'My God, you've done it!—a completely original expression that remains faithful to Mr. Wright's principles.'"

Vern Swaback, a Scottsdale architect who apprenticed with Wright in 1957, practiced with Taliesin Architects, and finally broke away to start his own practice more than twenty years later, remembers that Wright pointedly tried to discourage his followers from imitating him. For the second project he presented to the master, "I pulled out all the stops. It had this great, big prow of stone. Wright looked at it and said, 'This looks familiar enough to me. Next time let's see what *you* can do.'" Swaback insists that it wasn't Wright who installed the cult of worship around him. "It's always the disciples who create the church."

He wrote in his autobiography that the camp at Taliesin West belonged to the Arizona desert as though it had stood there during creation.

OPPOSITE PAGE: *The Arizona State Capitol Spire is most dramatic at dawn or dusk.*

The school has long been controversial because of its nearly exclusive reliance on Wrightian examples and principles. A professor of architecture at the University of Arizona once said, derisively, "The students virtually have to be deprogrammed once they leave there." On the other hand, the unique living arrangements at Taliesin West are a useful cornerstone in a young architect's education. On the day they arrive, the apprentices are issued a shepherd's tent and sent out to live in the desert behind Taliesin West; in their second or third years they will design and build more substantial "pavilions" to live in. The shelters don't deny or wall out nature; they participate in it. "It forces us to understand what's going on in the desert," one apprentice told me. It was such understanding that led Frank Lloyd Wright to create Taliesin West.

In 2005, the Frank Lloyd Wright Foundation Board negotiated a sweeping transformation of the fellowship's mission and operation. Change had become both "urgent and opportune," said Swaback, the board chairman. With no architectural revenues coming in, operating expenses for Taliesin West and the original Taliesin in Wisconsin had far outstripped income from tours and licensing agreements. Under the new mission, the two Taliesins are to become centers for scholarship, symposiums, and research, exploring issues of the twenty-first century in architecture, environment, and community. Casual visitors will still be welcomed, of course. But no further unbuilt Wright designs will be resurrected, and the cult of personality will, over time, likely wither. The new driving vision at the Taliesins is to contribute to a more sustainable planet—a logical extension of Frank Lloyd Wright's life and work.

"Frank Lloyd Wright believed that the architect should have a hand in shaping nature," Swaback said. "That's a noble notion." If the ideas that emerge from the Taliesins are radical and provocative, that would be perfectly in tune with its heritage. Nobody loved to prick the world's conscience more than Wright.

OPPOSITE PAGE: Apprentice shelters enjoy no plumbing or electricity, but they must harmonize with the environment.

LEFT AND RIGHT: The encircling ramp around the David Wright residence leads up to the roof, which can be used as an outdoor space. Wright labeled the David Wright design "How to Live in the Southwest."

CHAPTER FOUR

THE "EVER ADVANCING HUMAN THREAT"

"WE'VE HAD MORE CLIENTS who were concerned about my background with Wright than clients who came to us because of it," Swaback has told me. It was a surprisingly candid admission from an architect who profoundly admires his former teacher, but it confirms that Frank Lloyd Wright's lifelong role as maverick and outsider remains intact today.

Thanks to his seventy-year-long career and the dizzying spin of his personal life, Wright was more famous in much of the world than any other twentieth-century architect. But his German-born contemporary Mies van der Rohe wielded vastly more influence on the look of modern cities, from Tucson to Taipei. If you went to school or worked in an office building built anywhere in America or any industrialized country after 1950, chances are that it owed a debt to Mies' steel-and-glass boxes. His admirers would say this is because the Miesian aesthetic perfectly reflected the spirit of modern technology. His detractors would say this is because any talentless architect could copy Mies, and they all did.

"The ever advancing human threat to the integral beauty of Arizona might be avoided if the architect would only go to school to the Desert..."

Wright's style could never be successfully imitated, but his ideas have had some influence. Grady Gammage, Jr., a Phoenix lawyer and son of the university president who commissioned the Arizona State University auditorium, argues convincingly that Wright's vision of Broadacre City has been realized in Phoenix, more than in any other American city. Wright envisioned a sprawling, low-density city of one-acre residential lots punctuated with more intense, high-rise commercial zones, all served by an efficient highway system. Although no city planners consciously modeled Phoenix or its suburbs on Broadacre City—essentially, the metro area has been shaped by developers and free-market forces—it coincides almost eerily with Wright's ideal, at least as far as land use is concerned. He would (and he did) disdain most of its individual buildings.

Wright's ideals of honesty in materials and buildings that respect the landscape have not had widespread impact, because they run counter to American cultural impulses. We grow up in an environment in which materials are not what they pretend to be, from wood-grained vinyl to virtual reality. Deferring to Nature also cuts against the American grain; until very recently our entire history has been about transforming the land, forcing it to work for us, instead of discovering ways to work with it.

Still, there are more than a few Arizona buildings whose architects were influenced by Wright's way of gracefully slipping a building into the landscape, and we are fortunate to have them. Among the jewels are the 1988 Boyce Thompson Arboretum near the town of Superior, Arizona, designed by Tucson architect Les Wallach of Line and Space; and the 1984 Loews Ventana Canyon Resort in Tucson by architect Ken Frizzell of FHMB Inc. in San Francisco. Ventana Canyon, in fact, is nearly the unofficial realization of San-Marcos-in-the-Desert. Like the unbuilt hotel, the vertical corrugations of the concrete-block towers echo the ribbing of saguaros, and the entire 330,000-square-foot megalith bows in humility to the mountain towering behind—the resort building has an air of rugged permanence,

OPPOSITE PAGE: Frank Lloyd Wright, 1947, at Taliesin West.

but not a shred of arrogance. Both these buildings, like Taliesin West, show us how a dramatic landscape can inspire a dramatic building without the two competing for attention and thereby diminishing each other.

Wright deserves the last word on Arizona, not because of his prickly prose or the dozen-odd buildings he left us, but because the core of what he believed is so utterly right—right for the land and right for humanity. In his 1940 essay for *Arizona Highways*, he wrote:

> *The ever advancing human threat to the integral beauty of Arizona might be avoided if the architect would only go to school to the Desert in this sense and humbly learn harmonious contrasts or sympathetic treatments that would, thus, quietly, "belong" ….*
>
> *Is this organic abstraction, as expression, too difficult for us at this stage of our development? All right then. Cover up your walls, plant trees and vines and water them well. But plant trees and vines native to the condition here. Be quiet—will you—at any cost. Blot out your clumsy intrusions as you best can. It is the only apology you can make to Arizona.*

APPENDIX A: ARIZONA BUILDINGS BY FRANK LLOYD WRIGHT

Public Buildings

Arizona Biltmore, 2400 East Missouri Street, Phoenix, 602-955-6600, built 1928. Tours available.

Arizona State Capitol Spire, Frank Lloyd Wright Boulevard and Scottsdale Road, Scottsdale, designed 1957, built 2002.

First Christian Church, 6750 North Seventh Avenue, Phoenix, 602-246-9206, designed 1950, built 1971. Visitors welcome weekdays 8 a.m.–5 p.m.

Grady Gammage Memorial Auditorium, Arizona State University, Mill Avenue and Apache Road, Tempe, 480-965-0458, designed 1959, completed 1964. Tours available.

Taliesin West, 12621 Frank Lloyd Wright Boulevard, Scottsdale, 480-860-2700, built 1938–1959. Extensive schedule of guided tours year-round.

Private Residences

Adelman residence, Phoenix, 1951.

Boomer residence, Phoenix, 1953.

Carlson residence, Phoenix, 1950.

David Wright residence, Phoenix, 1950.

Jester/Pfeiffer residence, Scottsdale, designed 1938, built 1971.

Lykes residence, Phoenix, 1959.

Pauson residence, Phoenix, 1940 (burned down in 1941).

Pieper residence, Paradise Valley, 1952 (still exists, but much of Wright's original design has been altered).

Price residence, Paradise Valley, 1953.

APPENDIX B: OTHER BUILDINGS IN THE WEST BY FRANK LLOYD WRIGHT

California

Public Buildings

Anderton Court Shops, 333 North Rodeo Drive, Beverly Hills, 1952.

Barnsdall Art Park, 4800 Hollywood Boulevard, Olive Hill, Hollywood.
 "Hollyhock House," 1916–1921.
 Barnsdall Residence A, 1920.
 Barnsdall Residence B, 1921 (demolished 1954).

Ennis-Brown residence, 2655 Glendower Avenue, Hollywood, 1924.

Freeman residence, 1962 Glencoe Way, Hollywood, 1923 (now owned by University of Southern California).

Hanna House ("Honeycomb House"), 737 Frenchman's Road, Stanford University, Palo Alto, 1937.

Kundert Medical Clinic, 1106 Pacific Street, San Luis Obispo, 1956.

Marin County Civic Center, 3501 Civic Center Drive, San Raphael, 1957.

Marin County Post Office, San Raphael, 1957.

Pilgrim Congregational Church, 2850 Foothill Boulevard, Redding, commissioned 1958, built 1963.

V. C. Morris Gift Shop, 140 Maiden Lane, San Francisco, 1948.

Private Residences
Ablin residence, Bakersfield, 1958.
Bazett residence (Bazett-Frank residence), Hillsborough, commissioned 1939.
Berger residence, San Anselmo, 1950.
Buehler residence, Orinda, 1948.
Fawcett residence, Los Banos, 1955.
Feldman residence, Berkeley, built 1974.
Mathews residence, Atherton, 1950.
Millard residence ("La Miniatura"), Pasadena, 1923.
Oboler residence ("Eaglefeather") and gatehouse, Malibu, 1940.
Pearce residence, Bradbury, 1950.
Stewart residence, Montecito, 1909.
Storer residence, Hollywood, 1923.
Sturges residence, Brentwood Heights, 1939.
Walker residence, Carmel, 1948.
Walton residence, Modesto, 1957.

Idaho
Teater residence and studio, Bliss, 1952.

Montana
Bitter Root Inn, Stevensville, 1909.
Como Orchard Summer Colony, Darby, 1909 (only two cottages remain).
Lockridge Medical Clinic, Whitefish, 1958.

Oregon
Gordon residence, designed 1956, built 1963 (originally built in Wilsonville, later donated to Frank Lloyd Wright Building Conservancy and moved 24 miles to The Oregon Garden in Silverton).

New Mexico
Friedman residence ("The Fir Tree") and gatehouse, Pecos, 1945, 1952.
Pottery House, Santa Fe, designed 1942, built 1985.

Utah
Stromquist residence, Bountiful, 1958.

Washington
Brandes residence, Issaquah, 1952.
Griggs residence, Tacoma, 1946.
Tracy residence, Normandy Park, commissioned 1954.

Wyoming
Blair residence, Cody, 1952.

SUGGESTED READING

Gill, Brendan. *Many Masks: A Life of Frank Lloyd Wright*. New York: G. P. Putnam's Sons, 1987.
Legler, Dixie. *Frank Lloyd Wright: The Western Work*. San Francisco: Chronicle Books, 1999.
Pfeiffer, Bruce Brooks. *Frank Lloyd Wright Drawings*. New York: Harry N. Abrams, 1990.
Pfeiffer, Bruce Brooks, and David Larkin, eds. *Frank Lloyd Wright: Master Builder*. New York: Universe Publishing, 1997.